Heart
to Heart

Inspiring
Women
to go deeper with God

Heart
to Heart

Delighting in God's intimate love

Jeannette Barwick and Beverley Shepherd

Foreword by Jennifer Rees Larcombe

Front cover image: Artville: Don Bishop

Concept development, editing, design and production by CWR

Printed in Finland by WS Bookwell

ISBN: 1-85345-311-0

Contents

Meet the Women at Waverley Team

Jeannette Barwick, founder of Waverley's Ministry to Women, has long been committed to helping women apply biblical principles to their lives and relationships. In 1987, the first event for women was held at Waverley Abbey House and over the years the heart of Waverley's teaching for women has been shared around the world through seminars, writing and audio-cassettes. Jeannette also teaches on temperament differences and co-ordinates Selwyn Hughes' worldwide ministry.

Beth Clark, the most senior member of the team, is a lady whose life is steeped in the Scriptures. Her Bible Study has been ongoing for nearly 30 years and her workshops on Bible Meditation at Women at Waverley weekends are greatly prized. She has endeared herself to all who know her, not only by her humility and prayerfulness, but also by her remarkable ability to establish rapport with people of all ages.

Beverley Shepherd has been a team member for over 10 years. She is involved in varied and demanding work as a training consultant. The encouraging and equipping of Christians in the workplace is one of her passions, and she is an associate speaker for the London Institute of Contemporary Christianity headed by Mark Greene. She brings to the team verve and vitality as well as depth of biblical understanding, and is especially appreciated for her ability to relate biblical truth to contemporary issues, particularly as they impact women.

Nicky-Sue Leonard is a a gifted teacher and a relative newcomer to the team, bringing to it her expertise and experience as a CWR-trained counsellor and facilitator of post-abortion workshops based on Christian principles. For a number of years she has co-ordinated women's events at Waverley and around the UK. Apart from an expanding role as a speaker at women's events, she is increasingly involved in teaching on CWR's counselling courses.

Foreword

It was just before one of my regular 'Days Out' with God that the manuscript for this book arrived – so I took it with me. It blessed me profoundly!

Like an awful lot of other people I've met, I have always had a problem over knowing that God really loves me. Of course I know it in my head but I have to be reminded, periodically, to receive this knowledge into my heart! As a child I could only win my father's love and approval by behaving perfectly and I constantly have to fight my instinctive assumption that God's love has to be earned in the same way. The way this book explains how God loves us, 'just because He does' is so clear I've copied out a few passages and stuck them up, as reminders, on my kitchen wall!

At the core of our being we all have a longing to be loved personally, intimately and unconditionally – but human relationships can so often prove disappointing. When loneliness bites it is not always cheering to be told 'God loves you' because He seems to have such a vast number of children all over the world that we feel lost in a huge crowd of faceless nonentities. This book makes it blatantly obvious that God loves each one of us individually, not just as a father and friend, but as a romantic lover and adoring husband. Some of the insights the book gives us into what it means to be 'His Beloved' would sound startlingly fanciful and far-fetched if they were not so firmly rooted in Scripture. In fact this book's greatest strength is its balanced blend of biblical truth, human psychology and outrageous romance!

As I sat there, reading the manuscript, I found it all so releasing that I startled my snoozing dogs by shouting 'Yes!' when I reached this point; 'Above all else, our relationship with the Lord must be maintained as a loving relationship, not just a dutiful one'. How easily our love for Him can degenerate into a dull round of 'oughts and shoulds'! We all need a book like this to keep the romance alive.

No words could adequately recommend to you such an exquisite book – you'll just have to read it yourself to understand what I mean!

Jennifer Rees Larcombe

Introduction

'My beloved is mine, and I am His ...'
(Songs 2:16, KJV)

Everyone longs to be loved. It's one of the 'design features' of the product for which the Great Designer Himself is responsible. And the love that our hearts crave is a love that is personal, unconditional and eternally enduring. No one has ever loved us in this way, or ever could, except one, our beloved Lord Himself.

The theme *Heart to Heart* was first explored over two weekends for women at Waverley Abbey House. It addresses one of the most important aspects of Christian living: knowing how to open ourselves to the love of God, to delight in its richness and to experience its security. Those weekends were exciting and challenging times as we sought to hear God's heartbeat for us and His Church and found ourselves entering into a deeper, more intense and more real relationship with Him.

Now Beverley Shepherd has joined me in putting together this book to share with a wider audience some of the discoveries we made as we ministered together with the other members of the Women at Waverley team.

Over the years, we have had many appreciative and encouraging letters from women following our weekends at Waverley and, if there was a common thread to be perceived, it was that they had been enabled to move into a deeper relationship with God. It was for this reason that we chose the title for a series of books for women of *Inspiring Women to go Deeper with God*.

Our prayer is that as you take time out with God to read and reflect your way through this book, you will feel joyful, refreshed, spiritually invigorated and, above all, *loved*. At the end of each chapter there are questions for reflection, and I would like to suggest that you might also play tapes or CDs of songs and hymns that express your love to God and His to you. This can be a great aid to times of reflection.

The issues on which we focus affect not merely the head, but also the heart. It has been said that the distance between the head and the heart is the hardest and longest to travel. May it not be so for you. God's love is so powerful and profound that there is always more for us to experience and enter into. Hopefully, you will thrill as never before to the revelation of such a lover and the wonder of being His beloved.

Jeannette Barwick
Waverley Abbey House
March 2004

Chapter One

The Lover of my Soul

Jeannette Barwick

Adapted from talks given by Beth Clark and Nicky-Sue Leonard

'I have loved you with an everlasting love;
I have drawn you with loving-kindness.'

(Jer. 31:3)

The great God of the universe has been described by someone as the world's greatest lover. Perhaps you are surprised or even disconcerted by that description but that is exactly what God does best – He loves with a love that surpasses the greatest of human loves. Because of who He is, He is able to love us with a love that can conquer all our heart's antipathies and overwhelm all our reserve, our suspicion, our distrust.

Let's consider some of the statements we find in His Word, which come, as it were, from His own lips:

'I have loved you with an everlasting love;
    I have drawn you with loving-kindness.' (Jer. 31:3)

'You have stolen my heart, my sister, my bride;
    you have stolen my heart …
How delightful is your love, my sister, my bride!' (Songs 4:9–10)

Before going any further with this consideration, perhaps we need to pause and ask ourselves four questions.

1. Do you really believe that God loves you?
2. How do you see God?
3. Why does God love you?
4. How do you know that God loves you?

Take time to think and feel yourself towards answers to each of these questions and try to be as honest as you can. When the answers do come, perhaps you would like to write them down to pray about in your special times with the Lord. It will be interesting for you to see how these thoughts and feelings change over time as you discover more about God's love – and about yourself.

My colleague Nicky-Sue put the fourth of these questions, 'How do you know that God loves you?' to a number of women as part of her preparation to speak on the subject of God's love at a Waverley Weekend. The results of her 'mini-survey' were illuminating. The answers obviously came right from the heart, and were often accompanied by tears or other emotional reactions. Some had a beautiful simplicity: 'I know God loves me because He is with me whether I am faithful or faithless – His love is unconditional.' Overall, however, they suggest that many people do not believe that God loves them – although they don't doubt that, as a loving God, He loves others. Self-worth is a powerful concept in our culture, as the L'Oreal advertisements, with their 'Because I'm worth it!' punch line, show only too well. These beautiful women, with their unbelievably luxuriant tresses, may be convinced they deserve much but, sadly, too many people believe themselves unworthy of any of the good things of life, let alone the love of God. They are also painfully aware of the inadequacy of their love for God, when, really, what they need to know is how much they are loved by Him. This is the point of real change in the spiritual life.

Then, also, the answers showed that the image we each have of God has a powerful effect. Many of us find it difficult to come up with an answer to what He is like. We have several images of Him that are difficult to integrate, particularly because He 'appears' differently in the Old and New Testaments. The Bible, in fact, is rich in images of God, and this richness gives us some understanding of who and what He is, but certain images may resonate more powerfully with some of us than others. One thing that seems to colour strongly our perception of God is the relationship we have, or had, with our human father, for obvious reasons.

A woman whose father spent much of his time at home hidden behind the newspaper expressed, in counselling, her difficulty in seeing God as someone who was interested in her and wanted to engage with her. Obviously having a harsh and unloving father who is impossible to please or satisfy, would make it difficult to think of God as a kind, accepting, loving Father who encourages us in our weakness and foolishness. Such thinking indicates that, instead of seeing that we are made in His image, we try to make God in our image. We seek to bring Him within the realm of our understanding; without necessarily meaning to, we put Him in a box. At root, this is an attempt to wield control in the face of frightening incomprehension, when He is, of course, beyond human definition. We can know something of Him but beyond that is mystery and awe. He is 'like' so many things that we know, but He is so much more!

It is not surprising, given the nature of human love, that we should ask why God loves us like He does. The fact, however, is that there is no logical explanation. He loves because He loves. There is a passage in Deuteronomy 7:7–8 which reads: 'The LORD did not choose you and lavish his love on you because you were larger or greater than other nations, for you were the smallest of all nations! It was simply because the LORD loves you' (NLT). God chose the Israelites for no other reason than because He loved them. They had no special characteristics that would particularly attract His attention, nor were they better than the other nations. C.S. Lewis, musing on this matter, humorously suggested that the Egyptians were far more likely candidates at that particular time in history than the Israelites, and we can see that, from a human perspective, they had much more going for them. But they were not to be 'the chosen people' because, actually, God's love does not have anything to do with qualifications – it didn't then and it doesn't now. God simply chose to lavish His love upon the Israelites, and He has chosen to love you and me. God decides, God chooses, God offers His gift of love. He is, by His own free act, forever committed to His people.

Let's look at some passages where His commitment is expressed most beautifully:

> 'I will betroth you to me for ever;
>> I will betroth you in righteousness and justice,
>> in love and compassion.
> I will betroth you in faithfulness,
>> and you will acknowledge the LORD.' (Hosea 2:19–20)

And

> 'Can a mother forget the baby at her breast
>> and have no compassion on the child she has borne?
> Though she may forget,
>> I will not forget you!' (Isa. 49:15)

This is how God loves us! It has nothing to do with whether we are attractive, successful or lovable. There is not and never could be anything within us to evoke that love. He simply *chooses* to love us. It is an exercise of His goodness towards sinners who deserve the exact opposite. God's love is unsolicited, undeserved and unconditional.

One of the greatest texts in the New Testament, and certainly the easiest to remember, says quite simply: 'God is love' (1 John 4:16). Notice that it does not say God has love, or that God is loving, or that God is lovely. When it says 'God is love', it means that everything God does is motivated by love – it is the expression of His being. Whatever course He steers, love is always at the helm. It means that, behind every action, thought, consideration and purpose of the Almighty God, love is always in control. This is love in which we can have confidence, love we can trust.

The whole purpose behind God's revealing Himself to mankind in love is that we might see that His love is not just general but personal.

It was this truth that staggered the great John Wesley when he grasped fully the fact that God loved him *personally*. He talked about getting the 'me' into religion, and there can be no real understanding of how God loves until we realise that His love pervades the tiniest details of our lives and that He loves us personally.

The apostle Paul, who perhaps experienced God's love as much as, if not more powerfully than, any other person in Scripture, spoke of 'the Son of God, who loved me and gave himself for me' (Gal. 2:20). Twice here he used the word 'me' and that is the whole message of the love of God. It is not so much that He loved us from a distance but that He loved us so much that He came the distance to this earth in the Person of His Son, in order to reveal Himself to you and me. Moreover, that love took Jesus all the way to the cross to die for us so that we might receive the gift of eternal life (John 3:16).

Even me?

Human love, even at best, is conditional: it depends on finding something lovely or lovable in another and it is tied up with need satisfaction. But God loves differently. He loves the unlovely, those who hurt Him, who rebel constantly against Him and foolishly look for love in all the wrong places. How could He send His own Son to die for us, knowing how independent, ungrateful and mistrustful we can be? We can only conclude that God *is* love and that He will do whatever it takes for us to know His immeasurable love. His love is not dependent on our actions. He wants us because He loves us, not because He *needs* us. His love is not only pure, but constant and continual.

What gripped the men and women in the Welsh Revival of 1904 was a new perception of truth – they saw the love of God in a new light, no longer as an abstraction but as a fact. They were galvanised into opening their hearts to the great stream of love flowing from

God and they were swept along by it in the most powerful way. A hymn, by Robert Lowry, which was sung frequently in those days contains these poignant words:

> Here is love vast as the ocean,
> Loving kindness as the flood,
> When the Prince of life, our ransom
> Shed for us His precious blood.

Boundless love – no limits

The great preacher Spurgeon one Sunday morning cried out from his pulpit in the Metropolitan Tabernacle something along these lines: 'Come, you surveyors, and bring your measuring instruments and see if you can measure the love of God. It defies analysis, beggars description, leaps over all obstacles. How can we measure the immeasurable, how can we define the indefinable?' Similarly, the apostle Paul, writing to the Ephesians, fell to his knees praying that they 'may be able to comprehend with all the saints what is the width and length and depth and height – to know the love of Christ which passes knowledge …' (3:18–19, NKJV). The point behind these words is that the individual Christian mind cannot ever understand the vastness of God's love. It takes all the Church together even to begin to understand it. Of course, the attributes of His love are countless but here are just seven on which we can usefully focus. God's love is:

1. Infinite in its character (John 17:23)
2. Compelling in its power (2 Cor. 5:14–15)
3. Inseparable in its object (Rom. 8:35–37)
4. Individual in its choice (Gal. 2:20)
5. Unchanging in its purpose (John 13:1)
6. Everlasting in its duration (Jer. 31:3)

7.   Universal in its extent (John 3:16)

Boundless, matchless, wondrous love of God!

The lover of my soul

We are used to the concept of being loved for our qualities or attributes – our looks, our abilities, our resources, our achievements – but for our *soul* to be loved is something very different. That means our very being, the part that we mostly tend to keep hidden. What sort of lover could or would want to love our soul?

'Why is the soul precious?' we may also ask. First of all, because it was created by God and for God. It is that aspect of our being that distinguishes us from other forms of creation and enables us to relate to Him. He made us to bear His image, to be like Him both as spiritual beings and also as thinking, feeling and choosing beings and, in the incarnation of Jesus Christ, His identification with us was made complete. He became, for us, a man who was tempted in all things, like us, yet remained sinless.

Secondly, the soul is precious because it is eternal – it is destined to live forever, either in a relationship with God or outside of a relationship with God. How little this truth is grasped by those for whom this earthly life is all there is to care about, and how it changes everything when we gain that eternal perspective!

Thirdly, because the soul's salvation cost the Son of God everything. The price was not just the agony of death on Calvary's cross 2,000 years ago, but the far greater agony of necessary separation for a time from His beloved Father, as He took upon Himself the sins of the world. The world knows something of sacrifice but that kind of love is something else.

In spite of what I am

God's love is wholehearted and single-minded. What a challenging concept that is for us with our divided hearts and minds! God is a God of abundance who does nothing by halves. Some come to believe that God loves them a little but, as for revelling in His love, that is only for super saints. We need to realise that He does not have two kinds of love, one sort for mature believers and another for struggling saints.

If we tend to reject such extravagant love on the grounds of unworthiness, let us remember that God has chosen us and made us beautiful in His sight. 'For He has clothed me with garments of salvation, He has wrapped me with a robe of righteousness …' (Isa. 61:10, NASB).

Many of us at times reject God's love because we feel unworthy – and sometimes we prefer to condemn ourselves rather than accept His love, His forgiveness and His righteousness. We need to think hard about this and recognise the pride inherent in such a stance. If *we* punish ourselves for being unworthy, *we* remain in control, and therefore we are not coming before God in humble repentance. Our desire for control is an issue of the utmost importance because it goes all the way back to the primal sin committed by Adam and Eve that changed the course of human history. Their rebellion against God sprang from their desire to be free of His control. God offers to cover us in the righteousness of Christ if we truly repent. Let's accept it and walk in it with rejoicing hearts. We do not need to earn righteousness – and indeed we cannot; God's love for us is based entirely on what Jesus *has already done*. It is the love God has for Jesus, that love within the Trinity, that we enjoy – as a gift!

Another vital truth to be grasped is that God has also given us participation in the divine nature:

His divine power has given us everything we need for life and godliness through our knowledge of him who called us by his own glory and goodness. Through these he has given us his very great and precious promises, so that through them you may participate in the divine nature and escape the corruption in the world caused by evil desires.' (2 Pet. 1:3–4)

It is because of this that He can say: 'You have stolen my heart, my sister, my bride …' (Songs 4:9).

He loves first

We love because he first loved us. (1 John 4:19)

For he chose us in him before the creation of the world … In love he predestined us to be adopted as his sons through Jesus Christ … (Eph. 1:4–5)

This relationship cost Him everything.

This is how God showed his love among us: He sent his one and only Son into the world that we might live through him. (1 John 4:9)

That is how highly He prizes His relationship with us.

He didn't die so that we can have all our wishes granted and lead selfish lives. He didn't die to make us happy, but to make us holy. Some find this 'a hard saying', but it is a truth; He died for us to have a relationship with Him here on this earth and, thereafter, for eternity. Because it cost Him everything, let us not take His love lightly. Let us not use His love as a cover for conscious sin but allow it to transform us. Trusting Him is what it is all about.

At the cross we meet both the Judge and the Saviour – we cannot have one without the other. These aspects of God's love – justice and mercy – flow together. And having met God at the cross, we are called to live in the freedom of the resurrection, in relationship with the lover of our soul. This awesome God has chosen to love us because He is love. His love is unfailing. He covers our sinfulness with the righteousness of Christ; and He loves us as He loves His Son.

Questions for reflection

Looking back at the four questions I asked at the start of the chapter, are your answers different now?

- Do you really believe that God loves you?

- How do you see God?

- Why does God love you?

- How do you know that God loves you?

- How does this dawning of an understanding of God's love affect you in your day-to-day life?

- How does – or should – such understanding affect your attitudes, your behaviour, your relationships, your general mood, your sense of hope in this life?

- Do you know God's love as transforming love?

Chapter Two

Allured into the Desert

Beverley Shepherd

'Therefore I am now going to allure her;
I will lead her into the desert and speak tenderly to her.'

(Hosea 2:14)

'I will lead her into the desert' is God's promise, through Hosea, to His people Israel. It felt like a strange promise when God spoke these words to me, via a friend and mentor, several years ago – 'threat' would have seemed like a more appropriate word. The desert does not seem like an inviting or comfortable place in which to be led! In fact the words that come to mind when I see the word 'desert' are: lonely, vast, empty, monotonous, hard, unwelcoming, thirsty and desolate. Hence the thought of being led there evoked feelings of helplessness, vulnerability and isolation. Well could I identify with the character of Much-Afraid in Hannah Hurnard's book Hinds' Feet on High Places. Much-Afraid has been promised by the Shepherd that He will take her to the High Places. There her twisted crooked feet will be turned into hinds' feet and she will be able to leap joyfully over the mountains. The journey to the High Places is a hard one and she is given two silent companions – Sorrow and Suffering – as her guides. The detour through the desert challenges all she knows and believes about the Shepherd's character:

> Then one day the path turned a corner, and to her amazement and consternation she saw a great plain spread out beneath them. As far as the eye could see there seemed to be nothing but desert, an endless expanse of sand dunes, with not a tree in sight. … To the horror of Much-Afraid her two guides prepared to take the steep path downwards.
> She stopped dead and said to them, 'We mustn't go down there. The Shepherd has called me to the High Places. We must find some path which goes up, but certainly not down there.' But they made signs to her that she was to follow them down the steep pathway to the desert below.
> 'I can't go down there,' panted Much-Afraid, sick with shock and fear. 'He can never mean that – never! He called me to the High

Places, and this is an absolute contradiction of all that He promised.' She then lifted up her voice and called desperately, 'Shepherd, come to me. Oh, I need You. Come and help me.' In a moment He was there, standing beside her.

'Shepherd,' she said despairingly, 'I can't understand this. The guides You gave me say that we must go down there into that desert, turning right away from the High Places altogether. You don't mean that, do You? You can't contradict Yourself.' … He looked at her and answered very gently, 'That is the path Much-Afraid, and you are to go down there'. … 'Much-Afraid, do you love Me enough to accept the postponement and the apparent contradiction of the promise, and to go down there with Me into the desert?'[1]

Much-Afraid accepts that this is not a detour but 'en route' only because she loves the Shepherd and trusts that He is good. It is in the desert that each of us is faced with the question: 'Is God good and are His purposes towards me loving, whatever the seeming evidence to the contrary?' It's as if Satan is still asking the question he poses in Job 1:9: 'Does Job [or you and I] fear God for nothing?' Do we love God for the benefits He showers upon us or for who He is? It is in the desert that we find the answer to this question. It is here, where our various props and comforts are stripped away, that we are faced with the reality of our relationship with God. It is God's very love for us that leads us into the desert, away from all our activity and distractions, so that He can speak tenderly to us.

As we go through our Bibles we find that the desert is part of the life journey of many of God's people. Sometimes it is a journey through the actual desert as in Exodus, at other times it is a metaphorical desert as in Joseph's time in prison.

How then, does God cause us to enter the desert? The answer to this question is as varied as the different characters in the Bible:

- ▓ Abram – by God's direct command: 'Leave your country, your people and your father's household and go to the land I will show you' (Gen. 12:1).
- ▓ Rebekah – through marriage to Isaac: 'Then Rebekah and her maids got ready and mounted their camels and went back with the man' (Gen. 24:61).
- ▓ Joseph – through the hatred and jealousy of his brothers (Gen. 37:20) and later, through false accusation by Potiphar's wife (Gen. 39:16–18).
- ▓ Moses – through fear of being found out after he had killed an Egyptian (Exod. 2:14–15).
- ▓ The Israelites – by God's protection: 'For God said, "If they face war, they might change their minds and return to Egypt." So God led the people around by the desert road towards the Red Sea' (Exod. 13:17–18).
- ▓ Job – through family death, destruction of property, illness and misjudgment by 'friends' (book of Job).
- ▓ David – having to flee from Saul's jealousy, but it was also a place of preparation (1 Kings).
- ▓ Elijah – through fear of Jezebel and exhaustion: 'Elijah was afraid and ran for his life' (1 Kings 19:3).
- ▓ Jesus – was led by the Spirit: 'Jesus, full of the Holy Spirit, returned from the Jordan and was led by the Spirit in the desert, where for forty days he was tempted by the devil' (Luke 4:1–2).
- ▓ Paul – for a place of training and preparation (Gal. 1:17–18).

God uses the desert as a means of drawing us into closer relationship with Him and as a place of preparation for the things He is calling us to:

Humans assume that success can be the only legitimate goal in life. Actually, the desert may look more like failure, even death. In fact, it is preparation for richer living, deeper understanding of 'God's ways' … it is darkness, dryness and despair that open us to God's guidance, grace and goodness. [2]

The desert has three key characteristics that God can use to speak powerfully into our lives: silence, solitude and uncertainty. We are going to explore each one of these in turn to see how God uses them in our desert experience.

Silence

Silence is rarely silent. Switch off the TV or radio and you will hear the hum of traffic, the voices of your neighbours, the arguing of the children, the ticking of the clock, the rush of the wind, the drip of the tap, or your own breathing. Yet in the desert even these sounds are gradually stilled and we begin to hear the noise that is within – those voices that we have deliberately drowned out by activity and entertainment. Whose voices are they? There are three voices we can hear – our own, the devil's and that of God's Spirit.

1. Our own inner voices

In the silence we hear the voices of our self-pity, anger, hurt, loneliness and pain; and hearing them, we can no longer ignore their reality. In 1 Kings 19, following Jezebel's threats to take his life, Elijah flees into the desert and collapses under a broom tree. It's not long before those inner voices begin to surface:

'I have had enough'
'I am no better than my ancestors'
'I have been very zealous for the LORD God Almighty'
'I am the only one left'

'They are trying to kill me'

Exhaustion, pride, self-righteousness, self-pity, loneliness and fear – they are all there. What is God's reaction? Firstly, He lets it all come out – He knows that it has been buried and festering for far too long. Here, in the desert, with no one but God and His angel around, Elijah can safely give voice to all the mess that is inside him – several times over! God listens and He cares. He sends His angel to minister to Elijah's physical needs and then leads him further into the desert for 40 days – until he reaches Horeb, the mountain of God.

I like to imagine Elijah, with each step of that 40-day journey, shedding another piece of the angst that is inside him – gradually coming to a place of stillness and inner quiet before the Lord, even though he rehearses it all again (v.10) when he gets there!

Sometimes we long to hear from God, yet are so full of our inner voices that we cannot hear Him. There has to be a place in us where God's Word can be received before He will speak. 'Be still and know that I am God' (Psa. 46:10), is not a polite suggestion, it is a command! He is commanding the outer activism and inner monologue to stop. It may take a 40-day journey into the desert for us to begin to hear God.

When God speaks to Elijah He challenges the unreality in Elijah's thinking: 'Yet I reserve seven thousand in Israel – all whose knees have not bowed down to Baal and all whose mouths have not kissed him' (1 Kings 19:18), and gives him fresh vision for the future. God reminds Elijah of His call on his life.

2. The devil's voice
It was in the desert that Jesus was tempted by Satan (Luke 4:1–13).

'If you are the Son of God, tell this stone to become bread.'

'I will give you … if you worship me.'
'If you are the Son of God … test God.'

Jesus resists these temptations by speaking and obeying God's Word. Even in the desert there is a choice as to whom we will listen. This choice is portrayed in Psalm 1. Will we be like those who 'walk in the counsel of the wicked or stand in the way of sinners or sit in the seat of mockers' (Psa. 1:1)? Or will we follow the example of Jesus whose 'delight is in the law of the LORD, and on his law he meditates day and night' (Psa. 1:2)? Even in the desert we can be like a tree planted by streams of water if we have pushed our roots down deep into the Word of God. Jesus is not merely quoting texts at the devil – He is declaring the character of God. It is as we study the Word of God where God reveals His covenant love for His people, that we learn to trust that His loving purposes for us are so much better than anything the devil can offer.

3. The voice of God's Spirit

God plants His desires within each one of us – desires that, at the appointed time, He will bring to fruition. 'Delight yourself in the Lord and he will give you the desires of your heart' (Psa. 37:4). It is in the desert, just when we seem, like Much-Afraid, to be moving in the opposite direction, that God re-awakens the desires He has given us.

'Therefore I am now going to allure her; I will lead her into the desert and speak tenderly to her. There I will give her back her vineyards, and will make the Valley of Achor [a place of trouble] a door of hope.' (Hosea 2:14–15)

God has 'allured us into the desert' because He wants to speak tenderly to us, and in Hosea 2:14–23 we see tender words of:

▦	restoration	'I will give her back her vineyards.'
▦	encouragement	'I will make the Valley of Achor a door of hope.'
▦	renewal	'She will sing as in the days of her youth.'
▦	relationship	'You will call me "my husband".'
▦	cleansing	'I will remove the names of the Baals from her lips.'
▦	security	'… all may lie down in safety.'
▦	faithfulness	'I will betroth you to me for ever.'
▦	responsiveness	'In that day I will respond.'
▦	love	'I will show my love to the one I called "Not my loved one".'
▦	belonging	'You are my people.'

The desert is a place of preparation where we are strengthened to receive all that God has for us, and where He speaks tenderly to us and draws us into a deeper intimacy with Him.

Solitude

Many of us are apprehensive about solitude – we do not enjoy being alone. In 'aloneness' we come face to face with ourselves and with God. There is nowhere to hide and no one else to meet our needs.

Some years ago my young nephew was given one of these 'learning' toys – a plastic container with lots of differently shaped holes. He soon realised that the round brick would not go through the triangular hole and vice versa. Yet we seldom learn that other people are not designed to fit the God-shaped hole inside us – only God can fill that part of us. It is only when we have learned to be alone that we are fit company for others. Until then we will be demanding that they meet some need in us – a need that can only be met in God. In solitude, we take the risk of feeling the full extent of our emptiness and invite God to take His rightful place.

Show me how to approach my sense of being alone and cut off so that it may not be any longer a condition to be dreaded, but rather seen as a means to closer dependence upon you. Let my soul learn in solitude the lesson of your presence. [3]

Solitude also frees us from the patterns and pace of this world.

… solitude frees us, actually. This above all explains its primacy and priority among the disciplines. The normal course of day-to-day human interactions locks us into patterns of feeling, thought, and action that are geared to a world set against God. Nothing but solitude can allow the development of a freedom from the ingrained behaviours that hinder our integration into God's order … In solitude we find the physic distance, the perspective from which we can see, in the light of eternity, the created things that trap, worry, and oppress us. [4]

As we learn to embrace solitude we can find that it is far from lonely. Here we develop an intimacy with the Lord and delight in His company. 'I will show my love to the one I called "Not my loved one." I will say to those called "Not my people", "You are my people"; and they will say, "You are my God" ' (Hosea 2:23).

As our intimacy with the Lord deepens He brings, through prayer, other people into our solitude. A few years ago I was a Christian Union Guest on the OICCU mission at Oxford University. My role was to work with the college Christian Union as they arranged events in college where Christianity could be discussed in an informal setting and people encouraged to go along to the more formal evening meetings where a well-known evangelist would be speaking. In the college to which I had been assigned, the programme was very 'thin' and I had plenty of free time. I felt that God was asking me to go into my room and pray. I spent several hours every afternoon doing this and gradually I began to sense something of God's great love for the people of that college. It was as if He were bringing the whole college into my small solitary room. He caused me to weep for them as I have never wept for anyone outside of my immediate family. He also showed me what He was doing there and how I could work with Him – it was a week of miracles.

The other person God brings us into contact with in our solitude is ourselves! As we learn how much we are loved by God, and in the security of His embrace, we can dare to ask Him to show us who we really are.

When we are willing to wait in solitude and silent prayer before God, the Holy Spirit begins to re-centre our lives, picking through all the distracted fragments and confusion, to the heart of who we are, to the place where God's love waits to welcome us. There we wait in hope and longing for the unfolding of the great secret, kept in God's love – the secret of who we are, in the image of the One who created us.[5]

As we embrace solitude, we allow God to fill the God-shaped hole within us. It is then that are we free to move towards others with love, secure in our own identity, and desiring to bless them instead of demanding that they fill our emptiness.

Uncertainty

'By faith Abraham, when called to go to a place he would later receive as his inheritance, obeyed and went, even though he did not know where he was going.' (Heb. 11:8)

In the desert we come to know our complete helplessness, weakness and lostness. We have to walk by faith and not by sight. We have to trust God and not ourselves – we are out of control! Most of us hate being out of control – we want certainty.

In a Personal Development workshop some years ago, we were encouraged to draw a picture representing our life journey thus far. For the first part of my life I drew a motorway – it represented the clarity of my direction and the fastest route to my goals. In the desert, however, we lose all sense of direction and can end up wandering around in circles. Our maps are useless – there are no landmarks, no known way. Instead of a map we have a Guide – a Guide who cannot be commanded or hurried. The only claim we have on Him is His love. God is not ours to own or control, nor can we demand His presence. We trust, not in what He will do for us, but in who He is.

It was whilst in my own 'desert' time that I wrote the following:

There is No Map

It is dark and there is no map
No sense of purpose or direction.
I walk, but towards what end
Here in the Valley of the Shadow

I try to make rules and structures
And then stumble over some unseen boulder
What is the point of singing
Here in the Valley of the Shadow?

Hands reach out and touch mine
Full of warmth and compassion
Yet I walk alone and distant
In this Valley of the Shadow

In desperation I reach out
I scream in my anguish of lostness
And then I know Your strong arms around me
Carrying me through this shadowy vale.

I say 'through' in longing trust
That after the darkness there is light –
A dawn of life and new beginnings
I trust because there is no map
Here in the Valley of the Shadow
Beverley Shepherd

The uncertainty we face in the desert forces us to examine our faith. Where do we really place our trust? Is it truly in God or do we actually 'walk by sight' whilst claiming to be led by the Lord? 'Who among you fears the LORD and obeys the word of his servant? Let him who walks in the dark, who has no light, trust in the name of the LORD and rely on his God' (Isa. 50:10).

I love to dance, especially I love ballroom dancing. The waltz is a particularly intimate dance – so much so that when it was first introduced into this country 'nice' young ladies were expected to sit it out. When waltzing, the woman submits willingly to her partner's lead. He determines which steps they dance, which route around the room they will take and also gently halts their progress when there is a danger of colliding with another couple. The woman's role is to keep in time and to follow – she cannot see where they are going, only where they have been. Trusting your partner is key. When we face the uncertainty of the desert, Jesus says, 'Follow Me and keep time with Me – dance by faith, not by sight.' It is here that our faith in the Lord's leading and our trust in His love grows – we learn to lean on Him. 'Who is this coming up from the desert leaning on her lover?' (Songs 8:5).

My prayer for each of us is that the answer to this question is: 'It's me, Lord!'

Questions for reflection

■ What has been your experience of the 'desert'?

■ How did you enter the desert – some life event, illness, alluring ...?

■ When you are quiet, of what inner voices are you aware?

■ How might you build effective solitude into your life?

■ In what areas of your life are you facing uncertainty? How are you responding to this?

Notes
1. Hannah Hurnard, *Hind's Feet on High Places* © 1982. Used by permission of Kingsway Publications, Lottbridge Drove, Eastbourne.
2. James Houston, quoted in the preface of *Formed by the Desert* by Joyce Huggett (Eagle Publishing, 1997).
3. From *When Lonely, A Book of Private Prayer*, quoted in Paul Iles, *Touching the Far Corner* (Bible Society, 1996).
4. Dallas Willard, *The Spirit of the Disciplines* (Hodder & Stoughton, 1996).
5. David Runcorn, *Space for God* (Daybreak, 1990).

Chapter Three

The Beloved

Jeannette Barwick

'My beloved is mine and I am his.'

(Songs 2:16, TLB)

One of the aspects of the love of God, and one that is not often emphasised, is the intimate and romantic nature in the Godhead – the romantic element that lies at the heart of the Trinity. Many times in the Scriptures God refers to His redeemed people in romantic terms; again and again, in the older translations, they are referred to as His 'beloved'. What a romantic ring there is in that word! It's a pity that the translators of the New International Version dropped it from many passages of Scripture, deeming it, perhaps, to be old fashioned. I believe it still has a place in the modern world so I love to refer to our beloved Lord and think of us as His beloved people.

The Almighty loved the children of Israel and longed so much for a close relationship with them that He constantly pursued them and whenever they ran away from Him He ran after them. We are His present-day redeemed ones. Like Israel, we also are a people 'sought after' and 'pursued'. The God of the universe has gone to the utmost lengths to capture our hearts and He desires an intimate and romantic relationship with us.

Why is this romantic emphasis so often neglected?

Many Christians find the subject of intimacy uncomfortable and intimidating. Those who have had little experience of demonstrative love in their developmental years often find it difficult to think or talk in romantic terms. Their hearts have never felt the impact of close and intimate relationships and because of this they transfer the subject of intimacy to the head rather than the heart. This is often referred to in counselling circles as 'intellectualising' – using the head rather than the heart to deal with issues. We hold marriage preparation weekends at Waverley Abbey House and our experience is that sometimes, when the realisation dawns on an engaged couple of what intimacy in marriage really involves, one of them may find the thought of such closeness too threatening. He or she may feel fear of a relationship regarded as potentially stifling or suffocating. A few have actually withdrawn from their engagement or have needed specialist help to overcome the difficulty. The same sort of difficulty may be experienced by some Christians when it comes to discussing intimate and romantic relationships in relation to the Trinity.

A few years ago, an issue of the bimonthly devotional *Every Day with Jesus*, entitled *The Beloved*, took as its theme our love relationship with God. Interestingly, it had a great impact on the lives of many people, men and women alike, and while most readers loved it, some found it problematic. Over the two-month period many people were able to make tremendous advances in their relationship with God, breaking through to a deeper level of real intimacy and finding it possible to relate to Him in a much closer and more personal way. But others struggled with the whole thought of relating so intimately with God, not able to cope with the concept of a relationship that seemed too close for comfort. They also struggled with the use of sexual language and imagery.

When Charles Wesley composed his hymn beginning 'Jesus, Lover of my soul, let me to Thy bosom fly', it is said that his brother John remonstrated with him, protesting that it was irreverent and improper to address the Saviour in terms of such emotional intimacy. Charles fortunately disagreed and went ahead to set the words to music, and multitudes ever since have thrilled to that hymn, for its words have brought them face to face with the fact that Jesus is not just our Redeemer, but our lover also. Some Christians feel that while God can love, He is not a 'lover'. A lover means someone who woos and wins the heart and body, not just the mind. There is romanticism in the heart of God just as there is in our hearts, only it is so much stronger and more passionate – more so than we can ever imagine.

What is intimacy?

Intimacy is a relationship with another that flows from a depth of
knowledge and understanding that is shared by no one but the two
individuals. Intimacy always requires making choices and taking risks.
Intimacy reveals the real you that most people do not see. We are all
complex beings and no one can ever know us completely – except our
Lord. To develop an intimate relationship with God requires a
willingness to reveal ourselves. A dictionary defines 'intimate' as
'closely acquainted or associated, very familiar, as an intimate friend'.
Intimacy involves disclosure, which means revealing the real you –
your innermost self, your hidden thoughts, feelings and emotions.
Disclosures of this nature often emerge in the counselling situation
and, because the revealing of intimate information has the effect of
drawing you close to the trusted person and establishing a bond, it is
necessary for professional counselling to have very clear boundaries
and supervision procedures. A counsellor who moves beyond those
boundaries moves into dangerous territory.

However, the wonderful thing for us is that, the closer we move
towards our loving Lord in intimate relationship, the safer and more
secure we become. He is the One who knows all about us anyway
(Psa. 139). This may be an assumption, but in the New King James
Version of the Bible, the biblical word for intimacy is 'knowing',
suggesting loving intimacy. 'Adam knew Eve his wife, and she
conceived' (Gen. 4:1, NKJV). But contrast Adam's experience with
David's lustful encounter, of which the Bible says that David 'lay' with
Bathsheba (2 Sam. 11:4, NKJV). David shared a moment of passion
with Bathsheba, but he did not 'know' her, for they had no ongoing
relationship at that time. They were not intimate in the biblical sense
of the word.

God's desire for men and women, from the very beginning, has
been for us to know Him and to walk in intimate fellowship with

Him. He proved this by forming the body of the first man, Adam, with His own hands and breathing life into him face to face, rather than simply speaking him into existence as He had all other created things (Gen. 2:7). He did not distance Himself from Adam and Eve even after they had sinned. He still wanted to meet with them and be with them and He came to them in the Garden, as before; at that very time setting into motion His redemptive plan, designed to bring fallen man once again into the intimacy He had intended (Gen. 3:8ff). He wants to meet with us and relate to us with this same intimacy.

The apostle Paul understood God's desire and considered everything in his life a loss other than the privilege of knowing Christ. He wrote, 'But what things were gain to me, these I have counted loss for Christ. But indeed I also count all things loss for the excellence of the knowledge of Christ Jesus my Lord, for whom I have suffered the loss of all things … that I may know him …' (Phil. 3:7–10, NKJV).

Clearly, Paul was seeking a level of relationship with God that cannot be attained through intellectual activity, religious works or temporary emotional experiences. He was seeking intimacy and he wanted others too to know the breadth, length, depth and height of God's love (Eph. 3:18). Such intimacy does not just happen – it is something we must pursue.

God – a passionate lover

Some find it difficult to conceive of God as a passionate lover. But everywhere in Scripture He is seen as a God who yearns for a richly romantic relationship with His children. Consider, for example, how much sexual language is used in regard to God's relationship with His people – metaphors rich with sexual connotations. An example is Ezekiel, speaking in the sixth century BC, '… I … saw that you were old enough for love, I spread the corner of my garment over you and covered your nakedness. I gave you my solemn oath and entered into a covenant with you, declares the Sovereign LORD, and you became mine' (Ezek. 16:8).

The love story of God, unfolded in the Scriptures, makes the stories in millions of paperback romantic novels seem trite and unimaginative. Time and again in the Old Testament God pours out His heart through His prophets. God's description of His lover is painful in its humiliating detail:

> 'But you have lived as a prostitute with many lovers – would you now return to me?' declares the LORD. 'Look up to the barren heights and see. Is there any place where you have not been ravished? By the roadside you sat waiting for lovers, sat like a nomad in the desert. You have defiled the land with your prostitution and wickedness … you have the brazen look of a prostitute, you refuse to blush with shame.' (Jer. 3:1–3)

God's intention for His treacherous lover is even more staggering: 'How can I give you up, Israel? … My heart will not let me do it! My love for you is too strong' (Hosea 11:8, GNB). Incredibly powerful, forgiving and passionate love!

Why does God use sexual and romantic language to express His love for His people? Does this mean He is a sexual being? No. It is used because it brings home to us most graphically that He is passionate about His relationship with us. The Almighty loves with a love that throbs with passion. And the way He loves us is the way He wants us to love Him. Sexual language describes the most intimate union that human beings can experience, and God wants to relate to us in the closest possible way.

Dame Julian of Norwich was once given a series of revelations into the sufferings of Christ and the wonder of the gospel. She was taken into the heart of God and came away with this simple conclusion: 'We are not just the object of His care and concern – we are His lovers.'

Some traditional church catechisms suggest that we are created to know God, to love Him and to serve Him in this world and to be happy with Him forever in the next. Excellent words, but they do not convey the full truth – that God yearns to love and serve us and promises us the ultimate happiness of being enfolded eternally in His embrace.

The Song of Solomon

One of the greatest ever depictions of romantic relationships is in the Bible in the Song of Solomon, or Song of Songs as it is sometimes called, which, tragically, is held to be the least preached-upon portion of Scripture. One of the reasons for its inclusion in the Bible is that the Jewish people introduced readings from it into the Passover, the celebration of the Exodus from Egypt – one of the most awesome and majestic movements of God in the Old Testament. The event has been kept alive by re-enacting the Passover and telling the story over and over again but, at some point in Jewish history, the leaders in Israel came to realise that the story of the Exodus, marvellous and magnificent as it was, could, with constant retelling, become stale and end up being nothing more than a religious ritual. To protect against this danger they introduced into the Passover the reading of that romantic love story composed by King Solomon. Wise and insightful men, they believed that entering into the vocabulary of the Song of Solomon, the vocabulary of love, would enable the participating families to think not merely in terms of action but of romance. They believed it would transform their relationship with God and save them from becoming ritualistic in their approach to Him.

How we women enjoy hearing tales of true love! In the Song of Solomon, we can revel in the moving story of the Shulamite woman and her lover, the shepherd, and of their love which endured through temptation and opposition, a beautiful analogy of the love between Jesus and the bride of Christ. I would urge you to curl up sometime with this wonderful book and feast on the sweet words of the great lover of your soul, Jesus, our Beloved.

This story is like a passionate duet and it needs, of course, to be read in the cultural context of the day. Besides cultural obstacles, there can also be emotional obstacles to enjoying the Song of Solomon: some find it difficult to read because they're prudish and feel uncomfortable with the explicit nature of some of the language. For this reason, some preachers spiritualise it and say that the two breasts of the woman represent the Old and New Testaments, the two sections of the Bible! This is not, I am convinced, God's purpose in giving us this wonderful love story. It is for us to revel in, remembering the context of the day and enjoying its amazing language.

How then can we develop this closer love relationship with God? here are some specific steps we can take to developing intimacy which I have found helpful.

Steps to developing intimacy

1. See the Christian life in terms of relationship rather than ritual.

When we first encounter God's saving love, either through a dramatic conversion that happens in a moment, or in a gradual awareness of coming to faith, we may be overwhelmed by the fact that our souls have been invaded by our Beloved. We feel a passion within that may well be compared with the feelings we experience when we fall in love. But it is not unusual, as sometimes in human relationships, to find passion diminishing as time goes on. What we experienced as earth-shaking and soul-changing is now taken for granted. The freshness of our spiritual experience becomes stale. In the language of our Beloved in the book of Revelation, we 'have forsaken our first love' (Rev. 2:4). One modern paraphrase puts it like this: 'You don't love me like you used to.' We may preserve the importance of our conversion by regularly attending church, reading the Bible, praying and celebrating Communion, but the romantic feelings we once had towards our Lord are no longer there.

When this happens, it is not unusual for Christians to compensate for the loss of these romantic feelings by throwing themselves into more committee meetings, more spiritual projects and so on. How tragic it is to see a Christian who is more taken up with the endless round of Christian activity than with serving others out of a passionate love relationship with the Lord.

2. Focus more on what He has done for you than what you can do for Him.

The cross *has* to have an impact on us. The cross not only saves us but alerts us to how much we are loved by Christ. The central element of our Christian faith is what He has done for us, and it is the awareness of what He has done for us that turns our hearts. It's like an old mill that's out of use because the stream that turned the wheels has dried up. One day heavy rains fill again the mountain stream and the water flows down to the mill. As the waters reach the paddle wheels, the machinery turns again. It has to – it was made to work that way. So it is for us. As our hearts are flooded with the realisation of how much we are loved so we have to reach out and live for Him. We don't work to earn His love but we reach out and serve others because we are loved.

3. Seek to meet Him regularly in His Word and through prayer.

There is much that could be said here about these two most precious channels through which we can experience rich and real two-way communication with God but this is reserved for the later chapter 'The Language of Love' where they are explored in depth.

4. Realise that love needs to be nourished.

Love that is not nourished will diminish or die. A marriage counsellor recently told me she often talks to women who lament that their relationship with their husbands is not like it used to be. Closer questioning usually reveals that both are busy leading their own lives, perhaps one going out as the other comes in. Often no thought at all is ever given to making special 'together time' in their busyness. As the saying goes: 'Hello!' How can a love relationship be sustained without nourishment – spending time with each other, planning little treats together, giving preference to each other's desires.

So our love relationship with the Beloved will thrive when it is nourished, as Revelation chapter 3 shows. We can spend time with our precious Lord, enjoying each other's company. There are so many little ways to do this. When you arrange flowers receive them as from Him and offer the arrangement back to Him. When you enjoy a meal, remember He loved to share meals with His friends and invite Him to share the meal with you – this can be especially meaningful for those of us who live alone. A minister tells of a woman he visited who was dying. To encourage her, he suggested that a chair be placed beside her bed where she could imagine Jesus sitting. The day came when he was told that she had died. Was there anything of significance she had said before she died, he asked the nurse. 'Not really,' the nurse replied, 'but, funnily enough, just before the end she asked if the chair could be moved closer to her!'

Read the Song of Solomon regularly. As the Jewish leaders realised so many years ago, this wonderful story is there in the Bible to help us to keep our love relationship with our Beloved vibrant and fresh.

5. Deal with one of the biggest impediments to loving God – lack of trust.

In recent research amongst a large group of Christians, the question was asked, 'What is the greatest difficulty you face in your Christian life?' The common response was disappointment and, on further probing, many qualified this as disappointment with God – but that had to be wrung out of them!

Scriptural writer Oswald Chambers says the root of sin is the suspicion that God is not good. As we can see on reading Genesis 2, the first sin back there in the Garden of Eden arose out of doubt of God's goodness – if He were good, why would He deprive them of the fruit of the tree of the knowledge of good and evil? The serpent planted that doubt in Eve's mind and Eve took the bait, thinking she couldn't trust God's word. Satan's seduction of our hearts always comes in the form of offering us greater control through knowledge rather than the 'unknowing' of relationship.

It is difficult to love someone we do not trust. But, if we have any doubts of God's goodness, we only have to come back to the cross. A God who gave His life to be crucified for us has to be good. But, you might say, 'I can't trust. I have been betrayed and violated!' So was Jesus – on the cross, for your sake and mine! Ask Him for the grace to help you trust Him – He will neither leave you nor forsake you as others have and will. Open up your heart, and let Him in on your most secret thoughts and failures; you are accepted in the Beloved (Eph. 1:6), no matter what you have been through. He has plans to do you good and not harm, and to prosper you in all your ways for all of your days (Jer. 29:11).

6. Develop the vocabulary of love.

Words affect us and touch our souls. Precious Jesus, Loving Lord, I love you, Lord, and so on. Use phrases from Scripture such as, 'Draw me after you and let us run together!' (Songs 1:4, NASB). Selwyn Hughes speaks of a woman in his church in Yorkshire many years ago who was so in love with Jesus. At the weekly prayer meeting she would exclaim, 'Eee, Lord, we do love you!' and the passion in her voice would make the others present tingle. Someone else might say, 'Lord, I'm so glad we're an item'! The important thing is that you use your own language. While you are in the process of reading this book, find a way of expressing your love to God in a way you have not done before. Maybe write Him a letter or a poem or, if you are artistically inclined, paint or sketch your feelings. You could also play a CD or tape using the words of hymns or songs as an expression of your love. There's more on this subject in Chapter Four, 'The Language of Love'.

Our Lord's desire is for you. He made the choice to do whatever was necessary to win you and have you as His own. The word for desire in *Strong's Bible Concordance* carries the sense of stretching out after, longing for, running after, overflowing – like water. Our Beloved is stretching out after *you*, calling *you* to come and spend time with Him and get to know Him better. You can enjoy sweet fellowship with Him and, in time, become more like Him. If you wait for Him and persevere in His presence, you will find that He will flow over you with His Holy Spirit like a refreshing, cleansing stream. The Beloved takes great delight in *you*.

Brent Curtis and John Eldredge, in their book *The Sacred Romance*[1] point out that Scripture employs a wide range of metaphors to describe our relationship to God, and they place these in ascending order. Near the bottom, they say, we are seen as the clay and He as the Potter. Then, as we rise higher, we are described as the sheep and He as the Shepherd. Moving further upward, we are pictured as servants of whom He is the Master. Most Christians, they suggest, never get past this point. Moving up yet higher, we are described as God's children. But, they say, we can go up to a higher level still – the level where God calls us His 'friends'.

Is there anything higher? Yes, at the top of the scale there is a level of intimacy and fellowship awaiting us that those hearing of it for the first time can hardly take in –we are His lovers! The relationship the Trinity wants to have with us is most definitely a romantic one. God longs for a relationship where His passionate love for us is reciprocated by our romantic love for Him.

From my experience, there are different times in our lives when one or another of these metaphors is more relevant to us than any of the others. This is right and appropriate. So if, at this particular time in your life, the one of Potter and clay is most relevant, don't see this as indicating that your spiritual life is necessarily at a low ebb. On the other hand, do see the level of intimacy as desirable and attainable and something God desires for each one of us.

In Ephesians l, Paul makes it clear that we are not just noticed by God, we are *loved*: 'Long before he laid down earth's foundations, he had us in mind, had settled on us as the focus of his love, to be made whole and holy by his love … Long before we first heard of Christ and got our hopes up, he had his eye on us, had designs on us for glorious living …' (vv.4,11–12, *The Message*).

Now turn to the Song of Solomon and let the Beloved say to you: 'You have stolen my heart, my sister, my bride; you have stolen my heart … How delightful is your love, my sister, my bride!' (Songs 4:9–10).

Embrace these truths and hold them in your heart.

Questions for reflection

- What kind of relationship with us does God long for?

- Think through what best describes your relationship with God, from your point of view at the present time.

- Looking back over this chapter, what steps will you take to develop a closer love relationship with God?

- Spend time focusing on the two scriptures opposite selected from the hundreds in the Bible to help you engage with Jesus, the lover of your soul.

Notes

1. Brent Curtis and John Eldredge, *The Sacred Romance* (Nelson Publishers, 1998).

Chapter Four

The Language of Love

Beverley Shepherd
Adapted from a talk by Beth Clark

'Behold, you are fair, my love!
Behold, you are fair!
You have dove's eyes.'

(Songs 1:15, NKJV)

Communication is vital for any relationship. Without it a relationship doesn't develop and intimacy is avoided. God longs for relationship with us – He longs to come close to us and let us know how much He loves us – and He always looks for a response from us.

Although we know this, many of us are afraid of intimacy with God. We are like the Israelites in the days of the Exodus: '[The people] trembled with fear. They stayed at a distance and said to Moses, "Speak to us yourself and we will listen. But do not have God speak to us or we will die"' (Exod. 20:18–19). We sometimes prefer to hear from God via others rather than to spend time with Him alone. Why is that? For us, as for the Israelites, the answer, I believe, is fear. A friend of mine once asked me to help her understand why she would religiously make time to watch her favourite 'soap' on TV every day, and yet not find the time to be quiet with God. As we discussed it she came to the realisation that she was afraid of spending time with Him. What if He asked something of her that would put more pressure on her already busy schedule? What if He wanted to show her things about herself that she would far rather not know? What if He was looking for a depth of relationship that her frozen heart could not respond to? No, far easier to switch on the TV – it demanded nothing from her and didn't even mind if she fell asleep in front of it!

My friend is not alone – if we have a concept of God that sees Him as a demanding taskmaster or critical parent then we need to understand that we have believed a lie. As we repent of this false belief we can ask God to show us His love and give us the courage to approach Him. This is not to say that He will never point out areas that need to be changed, or ask us to help Him with some work He is undertaking, but always this is within the context of us being co-yoked with Him. As Jesus says:

'Are you tired? Worn out? Burned out on religion? Come to me. Get away with me and you'll recover your life. I'll show you how to take a real rest. Walk with me and work with me – watch how I do it. Learn the unforced rhythms of grace. I won't lay anything heavy or ill-fitting on you. Keep company with me and you'll learn to live freely and lightly.' (Matt. 11:28–30, *The Message*)

Once we have chosen to deepen our relationship with God, we need to realise that communication is a two-way process which involves both listening to God and talking with Him.

How does God communicate with us?

'In the past God spoke to our forefathers through the prophets at many times and in various ways, but in these last days He has spoken to us by his Son, whom he appointed heir of all things, and through whom he made the universe' (Heb. 1:1–2).

The good news is that God is not silent! He speaks through the prophets (the Old Testament), and through Jesus (the New Testament). We also know that God the Holy Spirit will help us to understand and apply these teachings (John 16:12–14).

I believe that God speaks directly to His people, but that we need wisdom to discern His voice and distinguish it from the voice of the enemy or the voice of our own internal desires. The way we obtain that wisdom is through reading God's Word and coming to know His revealed character. Imagine that someone is speaking to you about a mutual friend called Anne – a friend you have known for several years. The speaker tells you some things that Anne supposedly said. Without thinking, you respond, 'Anne would never say that.' What enables you to discern whether Anne would say such a thing? Surely it is the length and depth of your relationship with her. The same is true with God – our knowledge of God though the Bible, and the depth of our relationship with Him, enable us to discern if 'words' are truly from the Lord.

Many of us would claim that the Bible is the most important and valuable book ever written. Yet the amount we read it would give lie to that claim. A woman's husband was going off on a long trip and she decided that she would write to him every day to express her love for him and to keep him up to date with all that was happening at home. This she did, spending many hours and infinite care on these letters. When her husband returned she was helping him unpack his suitcase when she saw her letters beautifully tied in a bundle with red ribbon. She was deeply touched until, on picking up the bundle, she realised that not one of her letters had been opened and read. Imagine how she felt! I suspect God's feelings are similar when He sees our beautifully bound Bibles lying unopened and unread on our shelves!

There are five ways of listening to God's Word:

- Hearing it read out loud
- Reading it ourselves
- Studying it
- Memorising portions of it
- Meditating on it

Hearing

One of the most important parts of our church services is when God's Word is being read out, yet how often our minds can wander, or familiarity can mean that we don't really listen. Listening takes energy, as any counsellor will tell you. We have to actively participate in the process and discipline our minds to focus on what is being said. It is helpful to pray that God's Spirit will aid us in this! We are fortunate that the Bible is now available on tape and CD so that we can listen to it in our cars or around the house.

Reading

Beth's husband, Dennis Clark, had read the complete Bible 85 times when he died aged 61. No wonder he had an extraordinary grasp of God's character and salvation purposes for this world! There are many reading plans to help us read through the Bible; there are different translations and paraphrases to help our understanding – we are without excuse. If we really want a relationship with the living God, we will read His Book.

Studying

Any study is hard work, so why should we bother? Paul gives us the answer in 2 Timothy 3:16–17. 'All Scripture is God-breathed and is useful for teaching, rebuking, correcting and training in righteousness, so that the man [woman] of God may be thoroughly equipped for every good work.'

Do you want to be equipped for the work God to which has called you? God challenged me on this recently. I know that He has both called and gifted me as a speaker, and a few days ago I was reflecting on a talk given by another speaker that I had heard. The presentation was polished and the delivery engaging and yet, as I thought about the content, it seemed to me that he hadn't really said a great deal! God then pointed the finger at me: 'Bev, are you more concerned with presentation than content?' He showed me that the only point in my opening my mouth on a platform is if I have something worth saying. The only way I would have something worth saying is if I present God's thoughts and not my own. The only way I would know God's thoughts is if I study His Word! I believe this doesn't just apply to speakers and preachers – if any one of us wants to be equipped to live this life and do our work, we have to have read and studied the instruction manual.

When I purchased my laptop I also bought a 'Teach Yourself

Microsoft XP in 24 one-hour sessions' book. Filled with good intentions I took myself through the first two chapters and soon was able to do my letters and emails. The other chapters are still unread. Why? I had learned just enough to get by on! A good friend, whom I call on whenever I hit any IT problems, can get my machine to do all sorts of wonderful things that I never realised it was capable of. He has studied the manual and become an expert.

Good intentions are not what count in the end: we have a choice – do we want to live life to the full, or are we prepared to do just enough to get by?

Memorising

Why memorise Scripture when we have such easy access to it in written form? By memorising it we plant it more deeply into our minds and heart. Then, when God wants to bring it to our attention, He just has to hit the 'recall' button!

If you are not used to memorising verses, then start with a small passage, perhaps just one or two verses, for a week. Write it out and place cards with it on in various strategic places – your mirror, the microwave, etc, and say it out loud to yourself whenever you see the card. Soon you will have planted it into your memory. Then you can do the same with another passage the next week!

Meditating

Biblical meditation is the process of holding a phrase, verse or passage of Scripture in the mind, pondering it, continually contemplating it, dwelling upon it, viewing it from every angle of the imagination, until it begins to affect the deepest parts of one's being.

The deep meaning which lies beneath the word 'meditate', as used in the Bible, can best be understood by observing what happens in the digestive system of ruminant animals. These are animals (such as sheep, goats, cows, etc.) which 'chew the cud'. The animal bolts its food down and then later regurgitates it out of its stomach and back into its mouth. It does this several times, a process that enables the food to be thoroughly digested, whereupon it is absorbed into the animal's bloodstream, so becoming part of its life.

Rumination and meditation are parallel words. When a Christian takes a phrase or verse of Scripture and begins to meditate upon it, the power which is resident in God's Word is absorbed into his or her inner being, producing spiritual energy and faith.

So how do we meditate?

1. Begin by asking God to waken your ear to listen to what the Holy Spirit is saying in the quiet of your heart (Isa. 50:4–5).
2. Read the verses or portion (short to begin with) many times until you visualise the setting.
3. Listen to what the words are saying.
4. Listen to who is speaking in the passage.
5. Observe the reactions of those to whom the word is addressed.
6. Ask the Holy Spirit if the word applies to you. Quietly and gently He will speak.
7. Open up your heart to Him – it could be reassuring, convicting, encouraging, or it may reveal a wrong attitude towards God or another, or identify something to be avoided.
8. Write down what God says.
9. Pray it back to Him, asking for strength to obey.
10. Let the Holy Spirit work it out in your life.

Through this process the Word of God becomes part of you and is worked out in your life.

Our Response

How are we to respond to so great a love? How do we communicate our love to God?

1. Priority

'You shall have no other gods before me.' (Exod. 20:3)

This first commandment shows the priority we are to give to our relationship with God. 'Before' carries with it the sense of rivalry – there are to be no rivals to our commitment to Him. Without total commitment, no true intimacy is possible: this is true in our human relationships and also in our relationship with God. God offers us a loving and intimate relationship, but He specifies the basis for that relationship: covenantal commitment. It is truly 'for better, for worse, for richer, for poorer, in sickness and in health, to love and to worship, till death do us join'.

I recall the day that God challenged me to commit myself fully to Him. I had been a Christian for nearly ten years, but viewed my relationship with God as a contract: I kept the rules and He delivered wellbeing (according to my definition) and answered prayer. It was the lack of 'wellbeing' in my life that had led me to accuse God of not fulfilling His side of the bargain! His answer was to pull the rug out from under my feet: 'Bev, there never was a bargain or contract, only a covenant. Will you commit to Me in covenantal faithfulness, for better, for worse … till death do us join?' I knelt in the Prayer Room at Waverley Abbey House and prayed that prayer. I wish I could tell you that it was a moment of pure delight – it wasn't! It was a moment of desperation; I had nowhere else to go. Yet, as I was later to realise, God made those same vows to me, and knowing that we are bound together in covenantal commitment has been foundational to my growing intimacy with Him.

2. Totality

> 'Hear, O Israel: The LORD our God, the LORD is one. Love the LORD
> your God with all your heart and with all your soul and with all
> your strength. These commandments that I give you today are to
> be upon your hearts. Impress them on your children. Talk about
> them when you sit at home and when you walk along the road,
> when you lie down and when you get up.' (Deut. 6:4–6)

These verses are known as the *Shema* (Hebrew for 'Hear') and are
recited by pious Jews daily. Notice the flow of communication – we
are first to listen or hear what God says to us and then we are to speak
about it wherever we go. Have you ever noticed how those 'in love'
find a way of bringing the name of their loved one into the
conversation at every possible opportunity? It shows that their
beloved is constantly on their mind. 'For out of the overflow of the
heart the mouth speaks' (Matt. 12:34). Does my speech evidence that
the love of God fills my heart?

I had the privilege of listening to a Nigerian bishop being
interviewed. He had been visiting England for several weeks and was
asked what he had noticed about the UK Church. 'You are afraid to
name the name of Jesus,' was his unequivocal reply. Surely, I ask
myself, if I loved Jesus with *all* my heart, *all* my soul and *all* my
strength – the totality of this love would overflow into my
conversation with others!

3. Obedience

> 'As the Father has loved me, so have I loved you. Now remain in
> my love. If you obey my commands, you will remain in my love,

just as I have obeyed my Father's commands and remain in His love.' (John 15:9–10)

Jesus spells out for us the reality of loving God – if we love Him we will obey Him. Conversely, if we don't obey Him we don't love Him. We cannot even plead ignorance, for His commands are given to us in the Bible! If we love Him, we will 'hear' (listen, read, study, memorise and meditate) and obey.

There are times when I wish that obedience were an 'optional extra' in the Christian life, but Jesus gives a severe warning:

'Not everyone who says to me, "Lord, Lord," will enter the kingdom of heaven, but only he who does the will of my Father who is in heaven.' (Matt. 7:21)

Thankfully,

'The LORD is compassionate and gracious,
        slow to anger, abounding in love.
He will not always accuse,
        nor will he harbour his anger for ever;
he does not treat us as our sins deserve
        or repay us according to our iniquities.' (Psa. 103:8–10)

4. Gratitude

In Luke 7:36–50 the story is told of a sinful woman who washes Jesus' feet with her tears, dries them with her hair, kisses them and anoints them with perfume. Jesus praises the extravagance of her act, declaring that it demonstrates her great love – a love born out of gratitude. 'Therefore, I tell you, her many sins have been forgiven – for she loved much. But he who has been forgiven little loves little' (Luke 7:47).

In any relationship there is a danger that we take each other for granted. One way of ensuring that this does not happen is through expressed gratitude. As the psalmist puts it:

Praise the LORD, O my soul;
    all my inmost being, praise his holy name.
Praise the LORD, O my soul,
    and forget not all his benefits –
who forgives all your sins
    and heals all your diseases,
who redeems your life from the pit
    and crowns you with love and compassion,
who satisfies your desires with good things
    so that your youth is renewed like the eagle's. (Psalm 103:1–5)

5. Loving others

'The King will reply, "I tell you the truth, whatever you did for one of the least of these brothers of mine, you did for me."' (Matt. 25:40)

In this passage Jesus explains that love and compassion shown to others – through feeding the hungry, hospitality to strangers, clothing the naked, visiting the prisoners and looking after the sick – is, in reality, love shown to Him. Conversely, failure to love others is a failure to love Him.

We express our love for God by being His caring body in a hurting world. (This theme will be developed more fully in Chapter Six.)

As we noted at the beginning of this chapter, communication is vital for any relationship. If we truly want to deepen our relationship with God, we must learn to listen to Him, and then to respond in faithfulness, obedience and service. This is the language of love.

Questions for reflection

▣ What does reading the Bible mean to you?

▣ Does your speech indicate what is on your heart?

▣ How do you view your relationship with God – a contract, a covenant, a loose agreement …?

▣ In what areas of your life may the Lord be asking for more complete obedience?

▣ How do you express your gratitude to God?

Chapter Five

Prepared as a Bride

Beverley Shepherd

'I will betroth you to me for ever; I will betroth you in righteousness and justice, in love and compassion. I will betroth you in faithfulness, and you will acknowledge the LORD.'

(Hosea 2:19–20)

he good news is that being 'prepared as a bride' is for all of us – one day we all will be at the bridal feast of the Lamb. We, His Church, are Jesus' bride and are being prepared for that day. This life is merely the prologue – the title page on our eternal life. To understand what it means to be prepared as a bride we need to look at betrothal and wedding ceremonies in biblical times.

In Hebrew culture, betrothal was as binding as marriage and so was seen as a very significant event. We see this in the story of Joseph and Mary. When Joseph finds that Mary is with child he considers divorcing her (even though they have not actually gone through the marriage ceremony, nor have yet come together physically, they would be seen as a couple from the time of their betrothal).

Prior to the betrothal, how did a bride/groom choose a spouse? They didn't! Most marriages were arranged by the parents; for example in Genesis 21:21, Hagar chooses a bride for Ishmael and in Genesis 38:6 Judah selects Tamar for his eldest son, Ur. In Judges 14:2 Samson, having seen the Philistine woman (this is prior to Delilah) that he wants to marry, asks his parents to go and do the negotiating for him. Usually the betrothal was solemnised by an exchange of gifts. When the servant of Abraham comes to look for a bride for Isaac he bestows gifts on Rebekah's family at the point at which they agree to the betrothal (Gen. 24:53).

The period of betrothal ended with the marriage ceremony. A day would be fixed for the marriage to take place. The bride and groom were dressed in fine clothes – usually embroidered; the bridesmaids would be with the bride, while the groom had his companions. The bridegroom processed from his father's house to the house of the bride and then the bride was escorted back with her handmaidens to the groom's house where the ceremony took place. Usually this would be in the late afternoon and the bridal supper would take place in the evening. The bride was covered with a large canopy (we reflect this in some of our songs, such as 'His Banner Over Me is Love'). Then the bridegroom joined her under the canopy. There was blessing upon them and prayers for their future life by parents and friends. (In the story of Ruth this happened at the time that Boaz actually declared that he was going to take Ruth as his bride: the whole town prayed for them, for their fruitfulness and their life together.)

They would then go to the bride chamber where the marriage was consummated. The festivities and feasting could go on for a week. Is it any wonder that at the marriage in Cana the wine ran out! Marriage was not just about the bride and the groom – it was an event for the whole community.

We see some of these same elements in our relationship with Jesus. In Hosea 2:19–20 the Lord says, 'I will betroth you to me for ever; I will betroth you in righteousness and justice, in love and compassion. I will betroth you in faithfulness, and you will acknowledge the LORD.' To solemnise our betrothal we are given the Holy Spirit as a gift – the engagement ring we wear to declare that God is committed to us and is going to marry us. Yet there is a period of waiting – we are waiting for Jesus' return when He will come and claim His bride and escort her to His heavenly home.

The ten virgins

The story of the ten virgins (Matt. 25:1–13) is a story about waiting – waiting for the bridegroom to come. How are we to behave in a time of waiting?

'At that time the kingdom of heaven will be like ten virgins who took their lamps and went out to meet the bridegroom. Five of them were foolish and five were wise. The foolish ones took their lamps but did not take any oil with them. The wise, however, took oil in jars along with their lamps. The bridegroom was a long time

in coming and they all became drowsy and fell asleep.
[Bear in mind that they were expecting him late afternoon/early evening and we are told that he doesn't come until midnight.]
'At midnight the cry rang out: "Here's the bridegroom! Come out to meet him!"
'Then all the virgins woke up and trimmed their lamps. The foolish ones said to the wise, "Give us some of your oil; our lamps are going out."
'"No," they replied, "there may not be enough for both us and you. Instead, go to those who sell oil and buy some for yourselves."
'But while they were on their way to buy the oil, the bridegroom arrived. The virgins who were ready went in with him to the wedding banquet. And the door was shut.
'Later the others also came. "Sir! Sir!" they said "Open the door for us!"
'But he replied, "I tell you the truth. I don't know you."
'Therefore keep watch, because you do not know the day or the hour.'

In some ways this can seem quite a hard parable. These bridesmaids were meant to be friends and they are not sharing their oil – is that how real friends would behave? It is true that there might not be enough oil to go around as these lamps were not small – they were to light a procession, so a significant amount of oil would be needed. To understand the wise virgins' reaction we need to look at what the oil represents. It represents our preparation – our preparedness for the Bridegroom's coming. I cannot give you my preparation and you cannot give me yours. I can exhort you to prepare, I can encourage you as you prepare, but I can't do it for you. So my preparation is mine and your preparation is yours. All that God is weaving into me in terms of preparation in this life, I can't take out of me and give to you. He is going to weave into your life your own preparation, as you allow Him. God weaves things into our lives that we may not like, but when we think of it as our preparation for eternity we can more willingly co-operate.

But what happens when there is a delay? It is in the delays and disappointments of this life that we are tested and the reality of our relationship with God is evidenced. Why do I say that? Because to those who were not prepared, those who could not handle the delay, the bridegroom said, 'I don't know you.' There is something about the waiting that shows whether or not we know the Lord. It is in the waiting that the real agenda is highlighted. Am I looking to my own priorities and expecting the Bridegroom to work His timing into my agenda, or am I prepared to adapt to His? There is no point in my sitting there and saying, 'Well, actually, He should have been here at six o'clock.' We know from the Bible that God is never early or late. In this passage it says He was a long time in coming, but He has the right to set the timetable and it is we who have to adapt. If we are not prepared to adapt to God's timetable then what is that saying about our relationship with Him and His lordship in our life?

I don't find this easy. One of the great metaphors for my relationship with God is dancing and I am sometimes told by my dance partners that I get ahead of the music. Jesus also has to say to me, 'Bev, you are trying to go ahead of me. Keep in step. I am the One who is setting the pace here, not you, and My timing in your life is *My* timing and it is perfect.' Yet, I must admit that waiting is something that I am not good at.

Notice again the context for this passage; it is Jesus' teaching about the kingdom and His second coming. We could be tempted to say, 'Well, He has delayed 2,000 years so it is unlikely to be today or even tomorrow, so really I don't have to focus on it.' That is to be like the foolish virgins. They had only one priority for that day – to await the bridegroom – and they couldn't stay focused. Perhaps Jesus would say to us, 'The only priority you have in this life is to be prepared for My coming … What are you focusing on?'

I run training courses and among trainers there is an expression for when you are not fully prepared for a course – you 'wing it' and get through somehow. My preparation for a course is a sign of my commitment to that group and of the importance I place on them. We prepare for the things that we think are important. So again we can see why the bridegroom is saying, 'I never knew you.' It's a measure of our availability that we prepare. Preparation is not just about head knowledge, it's about weaving something deep into our lives, and that cannot be rushed.

I expect all the brides' attendants started out focused and excited about the arrival of the bridegroom. The difference between those who were considered wise and those labelled foolish was in their reaction to the delay. When there is a delay we are vulnerable to temptation – we may doubt God's word and think that the promise is void. Maybe the Bridegroom isn't coming at all … And the minute I think that, then it starts to make sense to do something other than wait.

> Waiting is not an interruption to a journey. It is an essential part of the journey itself. Having to wait involves submission. Waiting is an acknowledgement of our dependency. It exposes us to the illusion of our control. God is not to be hurried. Our life depends on the arrival of the living God. Waiting is a place of faithful obedience, ready to respond and serve the moment the need arises. It is not empty, but attentive and full of concentration on the will of the Master. [1]

We, like the virgins, are called to wait. The waiting is not an idle time, but a time of preparation – we are preparing to be Jesus' bride. The focus, however, is not on the wedding day, but on a shared eternity with our husband. Those of you that have been married know that although the whole focus and timetable before getting married is centred on the 'big day' – the real work starts after the honeymoon. So being a wife needs to be the focus of our waiting and preparation.

The woman in Proverbs 31

How do we learn to be a good wife? Proverbs 31 has much to teach us.

Many women find this a difficult passage. The woman in Proverbs 31:10–31 has been used to support a number of conflicting viewpoints. She has been used to advocate the career woman and held up as the working woman's model. She has been used as an example for the stay-at-home woman (who also works). It would seem that most women's reaction to Proverbs 31 is one of discouragement. Here is 'Superwoman' – an impossible role model whom I can't live up to. Let me encourage you to come fresh to this passage and to see what God would say to us through it. This chapter is dedicated by King Lemuel to his mother, recording the oracle she taught him and emphasising the role and significance of wise women. The inference is that if a man is to be a good and effective king or leader, then he needs to choose his wife carefully.

> A wife of noble character who can find?
>   She is worth far more than rubies.
> Her husband has full confidence in her
>   and lacks nothing of value.
> She brings him good, not harm,
>   all the days of her life.

She selects wool and flax
    and works with eager hands.
She is like the merchant ships
    bringing her food from afar.
She gets up while it is still dark;
    she provides food for her family
    and portions for her servant girls.
She considers a field and buys it;
    out of her earnings she plants a vineyard.
She sets about her work vigorously;
    her arms are strong for her tasks.
She sees that her trading is profitable,
    and her lamp does not go out at night.
In her hand she holds the distaff
    and grasps the spindle with her fingers.
She opens her arms to the poor
    and extends her hands to the needy.
When it snows, she has no fear for her household;
    for all of them are clothed in scarlet.
She makes coverings for her bed;
    she is clothed in fine linen and purple.
Her husband is respected at the city gate,
    where he takes his seat among the elders of the land.
She makes linen garments and sells them,
    and supplies the merchants with sashes.
She is clothed with strength and dignity;
    she can laugh at the days to come.
She speaks with wisdom
    and faithful instruction is on her tongue.
She watches over the affairs of her household
    and does not eat the bread of idleness.

Her children arise and call her blessed;
    her husband also, and he praises her:
'Many women do noble things,
    but you surpass them all.'
Charm is deceptive, and beauty is fleeting;
    but a woman who fears the LORD is to be praised.
Give her the reward she has earned,
    and let her works bring her praise at the city gate.

(Prov. 31:1,10–31)

The word *hayil*, translated as 'noble', is a word denoting worth. This is a capable woman (*hayil* implies ability and efficiency), a woman of moral worth. The word is most often used in the Old Testament of God – the helper of His people. It is also used of Ruth in Ruth 3:11. This is not a weak woman, but one who ably stands alongside her husband. She is good role model for us and not one to be daunted by. Let's study her in more detail.

Her relationship with her husband

He has full confidence in her (v.11). He lacks nothing of value (v.11). She brings him good, not harm, always (v.12). I think that is a wonderful expression. Am I bringing my earthly husband good not harm? (Though 'good' may mean that you have to be tough with him at times and challenge him.) He is respected by her, and by others (v.23).

Dr Scott Peck in *The Road Less Travelled*[1], pictures a loving relationship as one where both husband and wife have their own Everests to climb – and yet are each other's base camp and a source of supply to enable their spouse to climb. We don't have to climb their Everest for them, but we have to be the one who is encouraging them and supplying them and cheering them on, and they do the same for us. There is a sense in which this woman frees her husband to do what he is called to do, and he praises her (v.29).

Some of you are in relationships where you do not hear praise from your husband and you may even receive constant criticism instead. I remember some years ago, after my marriage had broken up, I went to the Sacred Dance Community in Dorset for a day. As part of that day we were given a stone and asked to imagine written on it words that had hurt us. At first I thought it was a bit of a strange exercise and then I sat down, and looked at my stone; and I knew that certain words my husband had said to me were on it. It was like a knife going through me. I had not realised the impact of those words until that moment. We were encouraged to put the stone at the foot of the cross and receive healing. It may be that for some of you, you need to let go of hurtful words and leave them with the Lord – and then hear what your heavenly Bridegroom says about who you are, because that is the truth and the truth will set you free.

Work

The woman in Proverbs 31 is a pre-industrial woman. She worked from home as did every other woman. In fact, as did most men. The home was the centre of family life and the unit of production. It was both dwelling place and factory. During the industrial revolution, home and work were separated and choices had to be made as to who stayed in one place and who went to the other. For many women their life goes in phases, particularly if they are married with children. The wisdom that is needed is the wisdom to know which phase you are in and to assess the priorities for that phase. We can easily, as women, put each other under condemnation because we have made differing choices. Each woman needs to be accountable in her own family and before God for the choices that she is making. (I recognise that some may not have a choice as they may be single parents or unable to work.)

The woman in Proverbs 31 works with eager hands (v.13); this is somebody who enjoys her work. We know from Genesis 3:17 that the context for work is cursed. Work itself is not cursed, but the ground is; we will face difficulties as we work: the photocopier will break down, your computer will crash and that person, who promised to phone you back, won't. Work, however, is a gift, whether it is work in the home or work outside the home – and this conviction will be evidenced by our attitude to it. In this passage we learn that this woman sets about her work vigorously (v.17) but is not a workaholic. In Hebrew culture relationship was put before the economics of profit and so work was relational.

Her arms are strong for the task (v.17). Perhaps this says something to us about the need to take responsibility for our own strength and wellbeing – are my arms strong for the work that God has called me to?

She sees that her trading is profitable (v.18) and watches over the affairs of her household; she is not idle (v.27). And so here the whole picture is of someone for whom work is purposeful, pleasurable and relational. She sets the tone for those around her. This is a lady who is heading up the household. If you are in charge of a team at work or if you are working with others, you will know how contagious your attitude to work is for those around you. Here you get a sense of somebody who is a joy to work with. This is not the ornamental leisured wife, nor is she the workaholic. She gets the balance right.

Money and generosity

She considers her use of money and for this she needs great wisdom. The use of our possessions and money says something about our trust in God as provider for both this life and the next. If I truly trust Him, then I can afford to be generous. This is a generous woman.

She provides for family and servants (v.15) and she opens her arms to the poor (v.20). Again there is a relational sense here. Opening her arms – this is a giving of herself and of her time. She extends her hands to the needy. Real caring has a short arm before it has a long arm. For me, it is far easier to write out a cheque and to send it for work on the other side of the world, than to think about what it means to be generous to my neighbour. The definition of hospitality is 'love of strangers'. In the Hebrew community, social care was exercised through the family. It was not somebody else's responsibility; it was seen as a part of every person's role.

Preparation

Her lamp does not go out at night (v.18). This is not about working through the night. This is the small lamp that was kept trimmed and filled with oil as a nightlight, so that if there was an emergency during the night a ready source of light was available from which you could light other lamps. This lady was ready and prepared to respond to the unexpected – unlike the foolish virgins we looked at earlier.

Clothing and looks

She is clothed in fine linen and purple (v.22). This is the appropriate dress for her position – dressing as who she is: the wife of a leader. We are daughters of the living God and we have royal robes, garments of many colours that we are to wear out into the world. We, too, can be clothed in the strength and dignity that comes from knowing that we are God's beloved daughters.

We live in an age that focuses on your dress size, your fashion choices and how old you look. We need to have a different focus and model something counter-cultural. Yet we also need to be wise in this because we work in a world that does look at our appearance – we don't want the way that we dress to be an obstacle in doing our work.

She is clothed with strength and dignity (v.25). Charm and beauty are not her focus because beauty is fleeting and charm can be used manipulatively.

Attitude and character

She has noble character we are told (vv.25,29). She is the personification of wisdom.

> The proverbs of Solomon son of David, king of Israel:
> for attaining wisdom and discipline;
>> for understanding words of insight;
> for acquiring a disciplined and prudent life,
>> doing what is right and just and fair;
> for giving prudence to the simple,
>> knowledge and discretion to the young –
> let the wise listen and add to their learning,
>> and let the discerning get guidance –
> for understanding proverbs and parables,
>> the sayings and riddles of the wise.
> The fear of the LORD is the beginning of knowledge,
>> but fools despise wisdom and discipline.'
>
> (Prov. 1:1–7)

'Wisdom' is offered to us from a variety of sources – friends, TV chat shows, the problem pages of magazines, self-help books – yet this woman knows where to start: the fear of the Lord. If we want wisdom for our lives then it is helpful to study the Wisdom literature in the Bible: Job, Proverbs and Ecclesiastes. Notice the words in Proverbs 1:3: 'disciplined, prudent'. It takes discipline to study God's Word and yet we cannot hope to speak wisely unless we have first listened to God's wisdom. This noble woman speaks with wisdom because she fears the Lord and so she can laugh at the days to come – she is not a fearful woman. I wouldn't have said that I was an anxious woman and yet the Lord has recently been highlighting my fears and challenging me to bring them to Him. What I have noticed is the way that He then helps me to deal with them: He underlines verses of Scripture, eg Romans 8:15, 'You did not receive a spirit that makes you a slave again to fear, but you received the Spirit of sonship. And by him we cry, "*Abba*, Father."' He reminds me of who I am in Him. It is God's Word that confronts the fears of this life. God's Word contains His wisdom and that is why this woman can laugh at the days to come: because she is listening to God and not to her fears.

The key to this woman is her fear of the Lord – this brings her praise and blessing from her husband, her children and at the city gate. In this life we may not receive praise and honour as she did, but we know that everything we do is seen by our heavenly Bridegroom and one day we will receive His 'Well done'. Yet we will only receive His 'Well done' if we use this time of 'waiting' as preparation – preparation for our roles in this life and our marriage in the life to come. Don't, I urge you, be shut out from the wedding banquet like the foolish virgins, because of wrong priorities.

Questions for reflection

▓ What is God using in your life to 'prepare you as a bride'?

▓ How do you respond to delays and disappointments?

▓ What do you find comforting about the woman in Proverbs 31?

▓ What do you find challenging about the woman in Proverbs 31?

- What meaning does 'the fear of the Lord' have for you?

- In what areas of your life do you currently need wisdom?

Notes
1. Dr M. Scott Peck, *The Road Less Travelled* (Random House, 1987).
2. From *Space for God* by David Runcorn (Daybreak, 1990).

Chapter Six

The Sacred Romance

Jeannette Barwick

'To him who loved us and washed us from our sins
in his own blood.'

(Revelation 1:5, NKJV)

I n this, the final chapter in our book, we return again to the focus
of our first chapter, that the greatest truth in our lives is that God
loves us. He loves us with an everlasting, boundless and sacrificial
love. Nothing that we did gave rise to it and nothing we can do can
extinguish it. He loves us, because He loves us, because He loves us.
Remember, He began the courtship, He initiated it, He began the
whole wondrous process – we love because He first loved us (1 John
4:19).

So great is His love for us and His desire that we love Him above
all others, that He allures us into the desert to deepen our dependency
on Him. There can be no other lovers for us because He is the only
One who can give us what our hearts long for – this was the focus of
Chapter Two.

Then we looked at the romantic aspect of love that is at the heart
of the Trinity. We know God loves us but we must allow Him to
become the One to whom we relate most intimately. We are called to
live as His beloved ones. We encouraged you to develop the language
of love through His Word and through prayer and then we looked, in
magnificent detail, at how we are being prepared as His bride.

God is a lover at heart and the relationship that exists at the heart
of the Trinity is a passionately loving one. Some years ago, Selwyn
Hughes came across this statement by the Australian theologian,
Broughton Knox. It transformed Selwyn's whole ministry and is now
fundamental to CWR's core teaching.

> The Father loves the Son and gives Him everything. The Son
> always does that which pleases the Father. The Spirit takes the
> things of the Son and shows them to us. We learn from the Trinity
> that Relationship is the essence of reality, and therefore is the
> essence of our existence. We also learn that the way this
> relationship should be expressed is by concern for others. Within

the Trinity itself there is a concern by the Persons of the Trinity for one another.

The essence of reality is relationship, not truth as many have been taught. Underlying the universe there is this deeply loving romantic purpose. This wonderful love relationship is totally 'other-centred' – meaning each Person of the Trinity is wholly centred on giving to the others and seeks nothing for Himself – and this spills over into a relationship with us. This love relationship is the model for the universe and it is our model for love; our model for life. The Christian life is not just a matter of carrying out certain duties and responsibilities – it is accepting the invitation to a romance. Duties and responsibilities are important, of course, but as G.K. Chesterton says in his book *Heretics*, 'Romance is the deepest thing in life: romance is deeper even than reality.'[1] It is.

So, if we can agree that the Christian life is meant to be a romance rather than a ritual in terms of our relationship with the Lord Jesus Christ, then the question we must ask is, 'How then shall we live?'

We must maintain a passionate love for the Lord

Above all else, our relationship with the Lord must be maintained as a loving relationship, not just a dutiful one. In the heart of every one of us lies a desire, a longing, for a Sacred Romance. It will not go away, in spite of our efforts over the years to anaesthetise or ignore it. Philosophers call this this heart yearning set within us, the longing for transcendence. It is the desire to be part of something larger than ourselves, to be part of something out of the ordinary that is good. This is what we experience, in a small but powerful way, when we celebrate something of national importance, such as when we get caught up in the excitement and preparation of a royal wedding. When the Queen celebrated her Jubilee there was a day's holiday. All over the country, people held street parties and other celebratory events. We had a party in our little road and neighbours who rarely spoke to one another had a great time together. It felt good to be part of this huge event. Just think of the mounting interest and excitement that happens during the World Cup and what happened during Live Aid; all because people have an opportunity to belong to something bigger than their own small world.

There is an awareness in the human heart of something going on that is bigger than ourselves. In the deepest part of our heart we long to be bound together in some common joyful purpose with others of like mind and spirit. We are connected to a larger story. As Christians, we actually live in a narrative, we live in story – existence has a story shape to it. We sense we are caught up in something bigger than ourselves and the Bible tells us what it is; the Christian life links us with God's larger story for mankind. We see all the minutiae of the story of our own lives, but every now and then we get hints or glimpses of the larger story God is writing , and these help us to transcend our own small world. Philosophers are perceptive but they talk in intellectual terms. What they call transcendence, we call romance. At the heart of this larger story there is a romance that resonates within every human heart and will not go away. It is the core of our spiritual journey.

The character and nature of God can be seen not only in His Word but in His creation. Take, for example, a glorious sunrise, a fresh carpet of golden daffodils, a snow-capped mountain or the rich hues of autumn. All these things God has built into His creation as inducements to draw us close to His heart. If I reflect on my most intimate meetings with God, I see an amazing variety of incidents – the fragrance of a lily, a verse of Scripture, the tears of a friend, my car running out of petrol, a picture drawn by my grandchild, a pair of swans nesting on the river bank. God has come to me in my ordinary everyday life in so many beautiful ways. I have received these touches with joy and gratitude and, at times, have felt overwhelmingly loved, but I know there is more to be shared and I continue seeking further ways to reciprocate and express my love to Him.

All these special messages that come to us, particularly through creation, are designed not just to be enjoyed for their own sake but to lift our eyes to our Beloved. Many times, though, we focus on the message rather than on the One from whom it came. It's almost like a bride being more interested in the dress, the wedding service and reception than in the bridegroom. Do we love creation more than the Creator? Jesus, referring to the fish which He had miraculously enabled Simon Peter to catch, asked him, 'Do you love me more than these?' He said it three times. 'Do you love me more than these?' (John 21:15–17). He wants our passionate love to be for Himself, He demands more from us than our love and appreciation of created things. We are not just student and Teacher, servant and Master, Father and child – all good, appropriate and intensely meaningful relationships in their way – but He wants us to be His lovers.

Romance lies at the heart of the universe. The larger story that God is writing is a love story and it is only when we see it as such that we get caught up in it. So our highest priority must be to maintain a passionate love for the Lord. In order to do this we must never forget that our initial focus should be not on what we can do for Him but what He has done for us. The central focus of the Christian life is always our indebtedness to Him for the love He has shown for us. If we get this wrong then we will quickly become casualties in the Christian life, working to be saved rather than working because we are saved.

Our love for Him is the direct consequence of His love for us and we must never allow ourselves to be moved from the fact that we love '*because* he first loved us' (1 John 4:19).

We must share His love with others

The Lord wants us to know Him so intimately that we can present Him to others and describe Him from personal experience – from having seen Him, from having heard His voice, from having felt His touch. So the second most important thing is: we must share His love with others.

What is the purpose of living? It is loving involvement with God, loving involvement with others, loving as we are loved. It is not enough that we know God's love in our own life and experience. That love must be passed on to others. The great challenge of the Christian life is not only to love God well, but to love others well. So, how do we love well? The best definition I have heard is given by the Christian psychologist, spiritual director and author of many books, Larry Crabb, and it is 'moving towards others without self-protection'. This means that, when we move towards another person, although we know they may reject us we can stand that because we are secure in God's love. So often we are more motivated by the fear of rejection than by the power of love.

God created us to be relational – first with Him and then with one another. As long as the relationship with Him takes top priority, we do well. But, all too often, our personal desires and frustrations begin to speak to us more convincingly than the voice of wisdom. Look around you – you'll see it everywhere, in families breaking up because of alcohol, unfaithfulness, pornography or just plain neglect; in children who've gone into the 'far country' of drugs, sex, abortion. And all these things can be seen within as well as outside the Christian community.

One of the characteristics of sin is its great subtlety. It creeps up on us almost without our knowing, especially at those times when we are most vulnerable because of some hurt, disappointment or loss, or when we're feeling tired or lonely. The Song of Solomon talks of the 'little foxes' that spoil the vines (2:15). When we allow the little foxes to invade our lives they can soon take up their abode in our vineyard and consume all the good fruit.

Nowhere in life does all this have more meaning than in the area of close relationships such as marriage and family, courtship, acquaintanceship and friendship. When we are hurt in our relationships, it is the easiest thing in the world to pull away in order to protect ourselves from further hurt, but all such self-protection – and let's be honest about this – is sin. It is sin because we violate one of the most important principles Jesus established when He commanded His disciples to love one another as He loved them.

Let's think again about what Larry Crabb said, that love is moving towards others without self-protection. If this true (and to me it seems to be so) then the converse is also true, that when we think more of ourselves than we do of others, we provide an entry point for those little foxes to do their worst. There is no doubt in my mind that one of the devil's most effective devices is to poison our relationships. I've found many times that, if he can't get at me personally, he will find a way of getting at me in one of my relationships. My instinct then is to withdraw and I end up not loving well.

It is possible to sell a cheap gospel, not clearly defining the cost of being committed to Christ. Paul says in Galatians 2:20, 'I have been crucified with Christ and I no longer live, but Christ lives in me. The life I live in the body, I live by faith in the Son of God, who loved me and gave himself for me.' In other words, my agenda and my rights were nailed to the cross with Christ when I committed my life to Him.

We love well when, although our hearts may be aching for comfort and consolation, we move towards others with the love with which the Lord is always moving towards us.

My friend Margaret is an example of one who loves well. She had an accident when she was working with young people and badly damaged some vertebrae in her neck, as a result of which she can no longer work and is often in considerable pain. She had loved to express her faith in practical acts of kindness but now she can no longer do many of those things she did for others. But, she says, 'I can still give them a smile for Jesus.'

We all need to be alert for opportunities to share the love of Jesus with others. In these days people are becoming more and more aware of a spiritual void, and situations around the world, tragic international incidents, impact us deeply and significantly. Just a few days after '9-11', my hairdresser said to me, 'I didn't think I believed in God but I must do, as I'm asking Him questions.' Let's be ready to respond to opportunities like that.

Luke 10:27 says, '"Love the Lord your God with all your heart and with all your soul and with all your strength and with all your mind"; and, "Love your neighbour as yourself."' The truth of the gospel is intended to free us to love God and others with just this wholeness.

What do our unsaved loved ones and friends see? Sometimes all they see is our frustration with other Christians or notice that we are more animated when we are with our Christian friends than when we are with them. No wonder they are not drawn to share our faith!

We must understand what it means to love ourselves

Our heart relationship with our Beloved is the key to having a healthy self-love. So, the third most important thing that will influence how we live is our understanding of what it means to love ourselves. A great many Christians are confused over the issue of self-love and consider it something we need to develop in a particular way rather than just acknowledge and enjoy. When we incline our souls in the direction of the Lord and love Him with all our hearts, and then share that love with others, we will really have no difficulty in loving ourselves. One follows the other as night follows day. If we do not get these steps in the right order, or we do not live them out, then much of what we do can become self-serving. We find ourselves doing things for others because we want them to like us. Our opportunity to minister to others turns into an opportunity to manipulate them.

Where is our sense of worth to be found? Is it in what other people think of us or is it in what we think of ourselves? I know many women who struggle with a low sense of worth. They are POLES – not people from Eastern Europe, but People Of Low Esteem! Are you a POLE? A woman said to me once, 'I'm not worthy of God's love.' I replied, 'No you're not! And I'm not either.' That's the truth of it. As has been said before, but will bear repeating, there is absolutely nothing that we can do to be *worthy* of God's love. He loves us purely because He is love.

If, like the woman I mentioned, you are holding on to a senseless belief of unworthiness, I entreat you to give it up NOW. Some actually hold on to that kind of wrong belief (what the Bible calls 'foolish thinking'), because it serves as an excuse not to move on with God and not to enter that close and loving relationship for which He longs. Oh, give it up, I implore you! Don't let self-pity come in and act like an anodyne, keeping you in that unnecessary and pitiful place. We can excuse ourselves and say, 'Oh, well, I'm just a terrible person. Look at all that's happened to me. I can't change.' Give it up now. As Jesus said in Luke 13:10 to the woman with the spirit of infirmity, so let Him say to you today, 'Woman, you are set free!'

Those who struggle with insecurity in their spiritual lives do so because they do not understand how deeply they are loved by God. Once that issue is settled, then love for others and love of self flow out from that understanding.

When God is our first love, we have a greater ability to love and give of ourselves to others. That way, our expectations are centred on God instead of the other person. I heard the story of an Irish priest who, while walking through his parish one day, saw an elderly peasant kneeling by the side of the road, praying. The priest was impressed at the sight and, quietly going up to the man, remarked, 'You must be very close to God.' The peasant looked up from his prayers, thought for a moment, and said, 'Yes, He's very fond of me.' The peasant was probably closer to God than most because he saw himself as the one who was loved.

There is no greater way of experiencing security in an insecure world than knowing we are part of a Sacred Romance. The God of the universe has gone to the utmost lengths to capture our hearts. George Herbert put it like this:

> My God, what is a heart
> That Thou shouldst it so eye and woo
> Powering upon it with all Thy art
> As if Thou had nothing else to do.

So drop your anchor into the depths of this reassuring and encouraging revelation. You are the object of God's romantic love; the Almighty passionately delights in you.

Brent Curtis and John Eldridge say that the Sacred Romance involves each of us in a journey of heroic proportions. It calls to us every moment of our lives. We may ask ourselves how God is wooing us in the midst of flat tyres, bounced cheques, rained-off picnics. What is He after, as we face cancer, sexual struggles and abandonment? We live, as we have acknowledged, with a longing to be loved and it is easy to seek the satisfaction of having that longing met in people and ways outside of God. We are reminded in 1 John 4:7 that love is from God. He is the only source of unfailing love and it is there our hope lies. He has left us the Holy Spirit who is our Comforter, and yet we often go for other comforters – just little things like popping a pill, chocolates, biscuits or alcohol – such paltry substitutes!

When we face trials our most common reaction is to say to God, 'Please get me out of this.' And when He doesn't, we resignedly ask, 'What do you want me to do?' Now we have another and probably more important question to ask – 'Where is the romance heading?' As we grow into the love of God and the freedom of our own hearts, we grow in our ability to reach out to God and draw what we need from Him.

Our Beloved has also set eternity in our hearts (Eccl. 3:11). This world is not our final home. We have received the gift of eternal life and we can't out-dream God. Paul says, 'No eye has seen, no ear has heard, no mind has conceived what God has prepared for those who love him' (1 Cor. 2:9).

The imagery of marriage pervades the entire Bible. It has been said elsewhere that it is a story that begins with a wedding and ends with a wedding. The imagery of a wedding feast is chosen by the Holy Spirit for a reason: the most intimate union of husband and wife on their wedding night conveys the depth of intimacy we will enjoy with our Lord in heaven. He is the Bridegroom and the Church is His bride. In the consummation of love, we shall know Him and be known by Him.

Just as intimacy with an earthly husband results in new life in the natural, so intimacy with our heavenly Bridegroom brings forth new life in the Spirit. As we come to know our Beloved Jesus in more intimate ways, fresh vision, insight and revelation will be birthed in our lives. We are anointed and endued with power by the Spirit in ways that will affect those around us.

If, as Broughton Knox says, 'relationship is the essence of reality', then nothing is more important in earth or heaven than developing a deep relationship with God and, in turn, a deep relationship with others. To do this effectively we must recognise that the Holy Spirit enters our lives to resource us with everything we need, to illuminate our lives so that the light of Jesus will shine through us to others who live in this dark and hurting world. It is to this most glorious truth that each one of us must commit ourselves.

Questions for reflection

- Reflect on the relationships in your life. What needs to be changed or improved? Are there any 'little foxes' that need to be driven out? Be specific in your prayers and honest before God.

- What do your unsaved friends and loved ones see in you?

- Are there any people with whom you could prayerfully share the love of Jesus?

- Where is your sense of worth found? Will you allow God to set you free from any wrong belief or self-pity?

- In the light of all you have read in this book, write down the steps you are going to take to ensure your love for God is maintained.

Notes
1. G.K. Chesterton, *Heretics* (Kessinger Publishing, 2003).

National Distributors

UK: (and countries not listed below)
CWR, Waverley Abbey House, Waverley Lane, Farnham, Surrey GU9 8EP.
Tel: (01252) 784700 Outside UK +44 1252 784700

AUSTRALIA: CMC Australasia, PO Box 519, Belmont, Victoria 3216.
Tel: (03) 5241 3288

CANADA: Cook Communications Ministries, PO Box 98, 55 Woodslee Avenue, Paris, Ontario.
Tel: 1800 263 2664

GHANA: Challenge Enterprises of Ghana, PO Box 5723, Accra.
Tel: (021) 222437/223249 Fax: (021) 226227

HONG KONG: Cross Communications Ltd, 1/F, 562A Nathan Road, Kowloon.
Tel: 2780 1188 Fax: 2770 6229

INDIA: Crystal Communications, 10-3-18/4/1, East Marredpalli, Secunderabad – 500026,
Andhra Pradesh.
Tel/Fax: (040) 27737145

KENYA: Keswick Books and Gifts Ltd, PO Box 10242, Nairobi.
Tel: (02) 331692/226047 Fax: (02) 728557

MALAYSIA: Salvation Book Centre (M) Sdn Bhd, 23 Jalan SS 2/64, 47300 Petaling Jaya, Selangor.
Tel: (03) 78766411/78766797 Fax: (03) 78757066/78756360

NEW ZEALAND: CMC Australasia, PO Box 36015, Lower Hutt.
Tel: 0800 449 408 Fax: 0800 449 049

NIGERIA: FBFM, Helen Baugh House, 96 St Finbarr's College Road, Akoka, Lagos.
Tel: (01) 7747429/4700218/825775/827264

PHILIPPINES: OMF Literature Inc, 776 Boni Avenue, Mandaluyong City.
Tel: (02) 531 2183 Fax: (02) 531 1960

SINGAPORE: Armour Publishing Pte Ltd, Block 203A Henderson Road,
11–06 Henderson Industrial Park, Singapore 159546.
Tel: 6 276 9976 Fax: 6 276 7564

SOUTH AFRICA: Struik Christian Books, 80 MacKenzie Street, PO Box 1144, Cape Town 8000.
Tel: (021) 462 4360 Fax: (021) 461 3612

SRI LANKA: Christombu Books, 27 Hospital Street, Colombo 1.
Tel: (01) 433142/328909

TANZANIA: CLC Christian Book Centre, PO Box 1384, Mkwepu Street, Dar es Salaam.
Tel/Fax (022) 2119439

ZIMBABWE: Word of Life Books, Shop 4, Memorial Building, 35 S Machel Avenue, Harare.
Tel: (04) 781305 Fax: (04) 774739

For email addresses, visit the CWR website: www.cwr.org.uk

CWR is a registered charity – number 294387

Day and Residential Courses
Counselling Training
Leadership Development
Biblical Study Courses
Regional Seminars
Ministry to Women
Daily Devotionals
Books and Videos
Conference Centre

Trusted all Over the World

CWR HAS GAINED A WORLDWIDE reputation as a centre of excellence for Bible-based training and resources. From our headquarters at Waverley Abbey House, Farnham, England, we have been serving God's people for 40 years with a vision to help apply God's Word to everyday life and relationships. The daily devotional *Every Day with Jesus* is read by over three-quarters of a million people in more than 150 countries, and our unique courses in biblical studies and pastoral care are respected all over the world. Waverley Abbey House provides a conference centre in a tranquil setting.

For free brochures on our seminars and courses, conference facilities, or a catalogue of CWR resources, please contact us at the following address. CWR, Waverley Abbey House, Waverley Lane, Farnham, Surrey GU9 8EP, UK

Telephone: **+44 (0)1252 784700**
Email: **mail@cwr.org.uk**
Website: **www.cwr.org.uk**

CWR CRUSADE FOR WORLD REVIVAL
Applying God's Word to everyday life and relationships